THE SMART APPROACH TO CONSIGNMENT STORE SUCCESS

How to Create

"WOW and $$$"

For Your New or Existing

Consignment Store

By Ron E. Hill

ISBN-10: 1496123654
ISBN-13: 978-1496123657

DEDICATION

I dedicate this book to my loving family

TABLE OF CONTENTS

ACKNOWLEDGMENTS

Kathy E. Hill

Melanie J. Hernandez

Jeremy S. Folliett

INTRODUCTION

Have you ever walked into a store and after looking around for a moment said or thought "WOW" because you were so impressed? That was our upscale household goods consignment store. The minute you walked in, the merchandise was sparkling clean and presented in an intentionally enticing manner. The well-lit and organized showroom immediately grabbed your attention. Everything, including the FREE fresh on premise baked chocolate chip cookies (available in the grocery dairy section), made a profound statement. It set the tone for what to expect from our store. And did it ever work. We were busy all the time helping regular and new customers and consigners. New consigners would even say "This is the store I want to bring my consignment to. I will make sure everything I bring in is clean like what you have in the store". That's when your store speaks for itself.

So what is the WOW factor and why consider it for your new or existing upscale household goods consignment store or other type of consignment business? It's the application of <u>tested and proven</u>

business practices that can make your store totally different from any other consignment store in your area. Applying these proven practices will make your consignment store so unique that it can literally drive your competition crazy.

What you are about to learn is how to implement these proven business practices to attract droves of consigners and spending customers consistently. These are exactly the same core business practices we used to create our very successful WOW upscale consignment store in the midst of numerous other consignment stores.

To help validate the importance of using tested and proven business practices, allow me to give a few examples of personal successful business experiences I have had, working in the corporate world and as a business owner.

One example of just how valuable tested and proven business practices can be was when I was employed by a cutting edge technology company, several years ago, that provided precision targeted direct mail marketing programs for major corporations. My responsibility was to contact major corporations and expose to them areas of their current targeted marketing programs that could be substantially improved without adding additional cost. In fact, what we had to offer actually cost far less when measured against the results we could consistently generate.

'

Keep in mind that normally, in the direct mail industry, obtaining a 1% to 2% response was the accepted norm. When we would state that we could achieve responses that were in the double digits, we of course were doubted. The reason we were doubted is because every other company offering direct mail marketing services were performing their services in about the same manner resulting in about the same 1% to 2% response results. We were initially perceived as just another one of those direct mail marketing companies. The only difference in their perception was our name.

Once we explained the business practices we would employ, based on our extensive development, testing, and actual applications, the intrigue we created for a test was always too much for the potential customer to pass up. When the test results were presented, the reaction was always the same.....big smiles and more business. In fact, boat loads of profitable business for the customer and us because of the tested and proven business practices.

One of my first experiences of learning the real value of tested and proven business practices occurred over 34 years ago involving a lawn and garden center that I started. The initial store size was 800 sq. ft. that eventually had to be expanded to 3400 sq. ft. plus a separate 2 acre nursery.

In addition to having a business plan that included rigid expansion criteria, the business plan also included guidelines for affixing pricing labels. Now putting the price label in a certain place on a product might sound off the wall but partially what resulted from doing so impressed my supplier of lawn and garden fertilizer and chemicals which was a major U.S. corporation. My sales were exceeding those of a nearby major nation-wide retailer. They were complaining about lost sales and my supplier wanted to know first-hand what we doing.

Now granted our pricing was matching and sometimes beating the nearby major nation-wide retailer because I had purchased an entire rail car of merchandise. In fact, I was their only independent retailer in the United States that ever purchased that much merchandise at one time. Three huge tractor trailer truck loads to be exact. In addition to our substantial inventory, my supplier sensed something else so they sent a team, including a film crew to my store. They also had another motive I learned later. They wanted to have actual documentation to show other retailers what they could do also if they ordered as much merchandise.

One of our marketing techniques they learned was placement of the pricing label.....always on the front of the merchandise in the upper right corner. You didn't have to turn the product upside down or around and around to see the price. It was easily visible on the shelf for every item. According to their statements, this was a first time experience and they were impressed. So impressed it became part of the documentary they created to show other retailers. So, is it important to establish and implement business practices that can enhance your business? My answer would be a resounding yes. A simple practice we applied gained national attention. Imagine what you can do to impress your local customers.

Even my experiences serving in the U.S. Navy echo the need to have a plan of action. Can you imagine the chaos there would be if the armed forces did not have tested and proven practices. I still remember, even though it was 57 years ago, how our drill instructor took 40 guys from all walks of life and shaped us into a well-disciplined team in 13 grueling weeks of repetition. We learned what it means to have structure and discipline. The instructor followed a plan that had been tested and proven and the results were always the same....a graduating group of men well equipped to perform the duties of military service.

These examples of exposure to and applying tested and proven practices throughout my life have instilled in me just how valuable they can be. There is no doubt that the successes I have enjoyed over the years as a corporate executive and personal business owner, are a direct result of not trying to reinvent the wheel but adhering to tested and proven practices. Your level of success will certainly be determined by the business practice decisions you elect to use to accomplish your goals.

MARKET ASSESSMENT REASONING

After spending more than five decades of working as a business owner and in the corporate world, I made a decision to retire and enjoy life so to say. Gone would be the weekly reports, running through the airports to catch a flight, being away from home, and so on. For a while it was great. I got up when I wanted, fished, always dressed casually, and in general just goofed off. But, there was something amiss....interaction with people. This was an everyday occurrence when I was working and now it was gone and I missed it. How could I bring this back into my daily routine without going back into the corporate world?

One day I was talking with my daughter in another city, who owned a consignment store, about doing something because I was basically bored. Without hesitation she said, "Why don't you open a consignment store"? I responded by saying my knowledge about consignment stores was close to zero. I had been in her store but never inquired about the operation of one. She said, "Don't worry about running one. I'll tell you what to do and even bring merchandise from my store to help you get started".

Long story short, I started to think about opening a household goods consignment store like hers and though her assistance would be available, my decision was to learn more about the consignment business including the stores in my area before moving forward. And that's where the rest of the story begins.....my approach of using years of successful business experiences before actually turning the open for business sign on because I knew everything had to be exactly right to be successful. The steps I took and business practices I implemented are what you are about to learn.

MARKET ASSESSMENT

Prior to the opening of our WOW upscale household goods consignment store, research was done to understand what was being offered in the marketplace. Every similar type business was visited including multiple visits to some. Mental and written notes were taken about each location. This included location, ease of entering/ exiting the location, size of the store, convenience of parking, merchandise offered, cleanliness, product displays, pricing, personnel, initial reaction once inside, terms of consignment, etc.. In essence, a clear reviewable list of what was currently being offered in the marketplace.

What resulted from the market assessment effort became very evident. There was no consignment store that actually focused on quality household merchandise. There was no consignment store that was a step above what you would expect when you entered the front door. They all seemed the same. Some of this and some of that for sale. There was no store that made the statement "WOW! This is a great place to shop". There was a niche in the marketplace that we could fill; an upscale quality household merchandise consignment store.

And that is exactly what we did. As the store grew in size and dollar volume, high end costume jewelry and genuine jewelry were added. Since the majority of our customers were women, jewelry became a great addition to the merchandise mix. During the several years we operated the store, numerous competitors opened, some just down the street from us and others nearby. Over time each of them closed. About 2 years ago we sold the store which is still open.

LEGALITY RESEARCH

Before you spend any money on your new venture, visit your local city hall. You need to clearly understand what the city policies are regarding a consignment store. This would include where and if stores are permitted, the type(s) of merchandise displays allowed outside the store and any license(s) that may be required and the costs. You need to know the type of advertising signs and other merchandising material city codes allow you to use. Your city hall will probably also let you know that your business name has to be registered with the state so you can obtain a tax ID number to pay state sales tax. Depending where you live there is a good chance you'll need the tax ID number to set up a business checking account.

GEOGRAPHIC RESEARCH

Your next step is to obtain a city map. These typically are available free from the Chamber of Commerce or city hall. Mark on the map where any other consignment or similar types of businesses are located. This will give you an idea of what areas can be considered for your consignment business. Keep in mind that main road arteries are normally the best because of the traffic volume and the exposure you will get. Consider ease of entering and exiting your location when you assess a potential location. Warehouses or storefronts off the beaten path, which could cost less to rent, could be considered but the down side is the amount of advertising you will have to do to regularly let the public know where you are located.

Other options that need to be considered include a store front that has front windows to expose your inventory to those walking or driving by, terms of the lease (a 2-3 year lease is the preferred), 800-1600 sq. ft. of display space in addition to an area in the back to be used for staging consignment, and potential options to expand if required. When the time comes to sign the lease, understand clearly whether you or the landlord is responsible for maintenance such as the air conditioning and heating system. If you are responsible, the cost could be significant (est. $4000.00-$6000.00).

The ideal situation is have the landlord responsible for repairs and replacement. The store front I chose was in a strip center on a main heavily traveled road that had six 800 sq. ft. stores, a double entrance parking lot with ample easy to pull into parking spots, and a large street side lighted marquise sign to place our signage. The landlord was responsible for all repairs other than our negligence. Over time, we expanded and occupied four of the six store fronts.

Up to this point, the only costs involved are a little gas for your vehicle and some of your time. You have acquired some legal criteria, necessary geographic data pertaining to potential sites, and exactly where your possible future competitors are located. This should be enough data to give you a reasonable indication as to whether or not your intended venture to open a WOW consignment store has potential.

THE BUSINESS PLAN

All too often individuals venture into the consignment store business with absolutely no guidelines to start and nurture their business. Many open their doors, start accepting the FREE inventory (love that FREE inventory). Some make it but a lot of them close their doors fairly quick. Where our store was located, several consignment stores opened. Today, not one of them is open. My assessment is that they lacked sufficient research and a business plan.

A business plan is the very foundation you need and a must if you truly want to succeed. If your plan is created with sound and logical business practices, you will quickly discover how important a tested and proven business plan is to your success. Applying my business plan criteria will give you the confidence of knowing, before you open for business, that you have a defined workable plan from day one to set up, open, operate, and possibly expand your "WOW" consignment store.

BUDGETING

Make a list to set a pre-determined dollar amount that you can comfortably afford monthly to cover the operating costs for rent, utilities, phone, internet, office supplies, security, etc. after you open the doors and for the first few months of operation. The pre-determined dollar amount should also include initial in-store set up costs. Estimated costs for the suggested initial in-store set up are listed in the back of the book.

The reason for this is quite obvious. Until your business is able to generate sufficient revenue to cover costs, it is critical to not be burdened financially and mentally from the beginning. Operating a business without undue stress is a lot more productive and a lot more fun.

As an example, suppose your total monthly operating expenses amount to $1500.00 and the consigner split agreement is 50/50. Since 50% of the sale is your portion, to cover expenses you need to have $3000.00 in sales monthly. That amounts to averaging $116.00 in sales per day (based on being open approximately 26 days per month). If your sales are sufficient to meet expenses right off the bat, that's great. In case that does not happen, because you pre-planned for the unexpected, business continues as usual with no undue stress. *A word of caution.* Whatever you do, refrain from taking a paycheck for a while. Build up your financial reserves to cover the unexpected.

When we signed the lease for our store and started to work painting, cleaning and in general preparing the store to set it up, some unexpected problems arose. This of course delayed our opening date. The clock was ticking because rent, electric and other expenses were being incurred. Because we set a budget and planned for the unexpected, it was not a problem. Granted, opening sooner would have been great but it all worked out because we had pre-planned. Later you will learn the approximate costs for initial fixtures, equipment and supplies that can be used to plug into your other expenses to create a budget.

INVENTORY

A key element to achieving sales to meet and exceed expenses is ample inventory. I visited a candle store one day and as I walked through the store I mentally added up the value of their inventory. I knew what the rent was because it was a location I had checked out. The dollar amount of the inventory was nowhere near what just the monthly rent was. You guessed it. They closed their doors 3 months after opening. What a waste of hard earned money. Be sure your finances and inventory can sustain the costs being incurred to operate your business. Also be sure your inventory appeals to the masses. Narrowing your inventory selection also narrows the available market and ultimately you sales volume. Be smart. Appeal to as many people as possible.

Whether you buy merchandise, use your own personal collected items, or advertise that you are currently accepting consignment for your Grand Opening, amass as much inventory as possible before you open for business. Make that first day of business for you and your customers a very exciting experience. Customers will be happy to have a new well put together business to visit and you will be smiling when the sales total is tallied for the day. Just a good way to start off.

Selecting and accepting inventory for a WOW consignment store involves extra discretion. Since a major component of the WOW concept is about having the very best merchandise, stock your store with quality. If any item is not up to the standards you have established do not accept it simply to fill the store.

As an example, each week I would visit homes to look at furniture and other items to be consigned. If the furniture was made with particle board I took a pass. We only accepted real wood furniture. I simply explained that though the furniture could be sold, our customers would not purchase it. If animals were present in the home and there was a lot of hair or an odor was detected on the furniture, I declined accepting it. First because of the work involved to try and clean and deodorize it, and secondly because of the possibility of a customer purchasing it being allergic to animals. Our goal was to have the very best inventory anywhere and we stuck to it.

CONSIGNMENT PROCEDURES

CONSIGNER CONTRACT AGREEMENT

Develop a one sided consigner contract agreement (8 1/2" x 11") and have an attorney go over it to be sure what is stipulated is within the law in your area and that both you and the consigner have protection. The agreement should include the commission split, length of consignment, discounts that will be applied such as 30% off after 30 days, 50% off after 60 days, disposition of consigned items after 60 days, payout day(s), responsibility of breakage, theft, etc.. Obtaining copies of competitor agreements can be helpful as a guideline.

The sheet with the terms of agreement can be at the bottom of the sheet that contains all the consigners information at the top of the sheet including their unique consigner number. Designating a consigner number is easy. The first consigner whose last name starts with "A" would be "A1". The next with a last name starting with "A" would be "A2" and so on. You should have ample room left to list the items to be consigned. Use columns to include the date their merchandise arrived, a brief description, date it was sold, amount due consigner, and a box for them to initial when paid for the sold and returned item(s). You keep the original and give the consigner a copy.

When the first original page is filled, use the second sheet (without the terms of agreement at the bottom) to continue adding consigned items for the same consigner. The two samples on the following two pages will give you a clear idea of what has been discussed.

ANY NAME CONSIGNMENT

1234 WOW DRIVE
ANYTOWN, USA 31333
(123)456-7890

Page: 1

Consigner Code: D4

Name: Jane Doe   Phone: (123) 555-5555

e-mail: Jado44@abc.com   Cell: (123) 555-7777

Address: 444 Post Road   City: Anytown   State: NY   Zip: 31332

	Date	Item Description	Initial Price	Sold Price	Date Sold	Amount Due	Date Paid	Initials
1	2/14/14	green sofa	300.00	300.00	3/10/14	150.00	3/15/14	
2	2/19/14	dinette table/4 chairs	425.00	297.50	4/1/14	148.75	4/15/14	
3	02/25/14	tiffany style table lamp	95.00					
4								
5								
6								
7								
8								
9								
10								
11								
12								
13								
14								
15								
16								

Consignment Terms Of Agreement

1.) When merchandise is sold it is on a 50/50 split between Anytime Consignment and the consigner.
2.) Payouts are made on the 1st and 15th of each month for merchandise sold up to 3 days prior to payout date.
3.) After 1 calendar month the merchandise is discounted 30%. After 2 calendar months, merchandise is discounted 50%.
4.) After 3 calendar months from date of merchandise arrival, unsold merchandise must be picked up or it will be available for donation at the store's discretion.
5.) Consigner must sign for all merchandise returns and payouts. Monies not collected by the consigner after 4 months will be forfeited.
6.) Any items that are not in excellent and safe condition cannot be accepted for consignment.
7.) Accumulated money in your account can be used towards store purchases at any time.
8.) Anytime Consignment cannot telephone consigner to advise when items are sold.
9.) Anytime Consignment is not responsible for articles lost due to fire, theft, water, shoplifting, damaged by smoke, handling, etc.
10.) Anytime Consignment has the right to offer 10% off on new merchandise priced at $25 or more.

Thank you for consigning with us

Consigner Signature: Date: /   /

ANY NAME CONSIGNMENT

1234 WOW DRIVE
ANYTOWN, USA 31333
(123)456-7890

Page: ___2___

Consigner Code: ___D4___

Name: Jane Doe   Phone: (123) 555-5555

e-mail: Jado44@abc.com   Cell: (123) 555-7777

Address: 444 Post Road   City: Anytown   State: NY   Zip: 31332

	Date	Item Description	Initial Price	Sold Price	Date Sold	Amount Due	Date Paid	Initials
1								
2								
3								
4								
5								
6								
7								
8								
9								
10								
11								
12								
13								
14								
15								
16								
17								
18								
19								
20								
21								
22								
23								
24								
25								
26								
27								
28								
29								
30								
31								
32								
33								
34								
35								

BOOKKEEPING SYSTEM

The bookkeeping system that I utilized was simple, effective and economical. It consisted of 3 ring hard bound binders to create an alphabetical bookkeeping system which contained the original signed consigner document.

This economical easy to set up system is an important key to operating your business. When a regular consigner comes in with more merchandise, you simply go the binder that contains their agreement, add the new items and make them a copy if requested. If they fill up the first page, you simply add another sheet and label it Page 2. The consigner's page number goes on the sales ticket as well so you can easily reference where to look when the item is sold and recorded on the consigner's sheet. We had several consigners who had accumulated many pages over time. This was because they used consignment as a means to make extra money. We'll talk about this later in the section Merchandise Resources.

Since these binders contain critical information, always keep them in a safe place. If you lose them, you have a major problem. Remember, should there ever be a need for legal action; you must have the original document. Our binders and some other valuables were placed and locked in an upright fire proof safe every night. It would be just short of an utter nightmare to try and recreate every consigner document. Note: There are software programs you can purchase if your preference is to have an electronic system.

DETERMINE CORE INVENTORY

Determine what the core inventory for the store will be. Maybe it will be upscale household merchandise, or just an assortment of mixed merchandise, or an inventory of merchandise for the do-it-yourself person. Whatever the decision is, stick with it. You will find by doing so, in time your knowledge skills will be greatly enhanced. It's a great way to build a reputation that your customers will quickly realize, respect, and rely on.

Offering clean varied inventory at a price significantly less than new attracts all types of people. Balance your inventory so there is something for those who are well to do and those who may have less to spend. Because of our WOW approach regarding the quality of inventory, we attracted many very well to do customers and consigners. Our store had an atmosphere they related to yet was not out of place for those who had less.

In addition to focusing on your core inventory, take advantage of the holidays such as Christmas, Halloween and Thanksgiving. Only accept items for these holidays that are unique, not your nickel and dime run of the mill items. For Christmas start accepting merchandise the latter part of November and then discount unsold items about a week to 10 days before Christmas. For Halloween and Thanksgiving accept merchandise three to four weeks before the holiday. Discount items a week before the holiday. Be sure to let consigners know your discount and return policies for each holiday.

ACCEPTING CONSIGNMENT
Establish procedures for accepting consignment. This includes days/hours for acceptance and the condition of the items. For instance, if your store is going to be meticulous and you don't want to spend a lot of time cleaning the merchandise before displaying it, then you need to advise your potential consigners. This can be done verbally or by the use of signage that conveys the stipulations for acceptance. There will always be isolated cases to deal with but the amount of time that can be conserved to use toward serving your customers can be substantial if you eliminate as much cleaning detail work as possible.

We tried our best to eliminate consignment coming in on Saturdays because it was usually our biggest sales day of the week. Basically we curtailed the amount coming in Saturday but we still accepted some because we had good customers that only had Saturday to bring it in. Surprisingly, a lot of it got sold off the sidewalk before it ever entered the store. Opportunities pop up. Take advantage of them.

HANDLING REVENUE

Whether you work by yourself or have employees, procedures to ensure proper handling, processing, and verification of cash, checks, and credit card transactions must be followed. At the end of each day, the total dollar sales for the day should exactly match the money and checks in the register and credit card receipts. When a check is accepted, be sure to get a driver's license number or other trackable information. Deposit all checks as soon as possible to ensure they clear. When processing a credit card, always double check the amount that is entered. It is easy to miss a number when entering the amount (example $4.00 rather than $40.00). Simple errors can be costly and if you are unfamiliar with the customer, trying to track them down could be quite difficult.

Another suggestion pertaining to credit cards is: DO NOT post a sign stating a minimum on the dollar amount for credit card purchases. Many people don't carry cash or a check book and if their purchase is say $7.45 and your minimum is $10.00, you will lose the sale and irritate the customer all over a few cents charge from the company that processes your credit transactions. A wise person once told me not to focus on the money. Make your focus the satisfaction of the customer. By doing so he said, "You will be absolutely astonished how much money you can make". I can tell you from personal experience that his words of advice are ever so true.

CUSTOMER INTERACTION POLICY
CUSTOMER VALUE

Customers are the most valuable asset of your business. How you treat them from the time they enter your business, while they are in your business, and even after the sale will definitely determine your success or failure. Courteous genuine concern to assist the customer can make your business stand out in numerous ways. Remember, people deal with people every day and if the experience is more than what is usually expected, they will come back again and again. Develop an interaction policy that projects a consistent professional and pleasant WOW experience with customers. A big smile and pleasant exchanges can do miracles. Let them know how appreciative you are that they are your customer.

Pleasing our customers was utmost to us. We bought a small cookie oven and throughout each day baked chocolate chip cookies using store bought ready to bake. The fantastic aroma permeated the entire store. The finished cookies were placed on a decorative plate just as you entered the store. Every customer who ate a cookie enjoyed it so much. When they brought their friends to the store, often the first words out of their mouth were "You have got to try their chocolate chip cookies". This added WOW value for the customer became such a big hit that even today, the store we owned that we sold, is still offering fresh baked chocolate chip cookies.

HONESTY and INTEGRITY

There is absolutely no excuse to not be honest. And when dealing with your customers, honesty is paramount. On one occasion, an elderly consigner, who had been bringing in a considerable amount of really nice consignment, stopped by with some items she said were her daughter's. At the time we were busy so we told her we would tag it (put a consigner number on it) and get to it later in the day.

That afternoon we started working on the items one of them being a small jewelry chest. As usual we started cleaning and when we opened the drawers we were shocked. Inside was loads of genuine jewelry with rubies, diamonds, sapphires, emeralds and solid gold necklaces and bracelets. The estimated cost was over $30,000.00. We bagged all the jewelry, put it in our safe, and then called the consigner asking her to stop by the store. When she arrived and we showed her what we had found, her comment was "My daughter must have forgotten about this. Thank you". She was very appreciative and I'm quite sure that in her mind she undoubtedly knew that the business she was dealing with was an honest business.

Another example of how honesty can effect a business involved a beautiful diamond ring we received for consignment. We were told the original cost was several thousand dollars. I needed some professional advice so I took the ring to a local jeweler to inquire about its value. I was told the shape of the diamonds was not a desired shape and I was offered only a few hundred dollars for it. Needless to say I declined the offer and took it to another jeweler who said it was a stunning ring and was worth several thousand dollars. We sold it to one of our customers based on the pricing advice of the second jeweler. Bottom line, the second jeweler became a trusted go to for advice business, someone to recommend to our customers, and over time a trusted friend. The first jeweler never got our recommendation.

See also

- Business Attire
- Promptness

BRANDING AND IMAGE

BRANDING

For all advertising, develop signage, business cards, and other marketing pieces that are indicative of your business. It's so important to develop branding recognition. Major retailers do it for a reason. Follow their lead. As an example, the sign lettering and wording on our truck, magnetic vehicle signs, and business cards were identical. There was no mixed messaging.

BUSINESS IMAGE

To ensure clarity and image projection is consistent with the business, decide what colors and graphics you want to use for the store decor. Choose colors that bring an element of warmth to the store's interior. Doing so will help your display pieces and the merchandise on them to stand out.

BUSINESS ATTIRE

The saying "Dress for Success" means look like you are a professional and that you are serious about your responsibilities. Often first impressions of personal appearance create in a person's mind what they can expect from the business. Though the typical consignment store is usually classified as a casual business, make it a company policy to dress according to the image you want to project.

STORE CLEANLINESS

Cleaning may not sound important but if you want the entire shopping visit a pleasant experience be serious about it. The shopping experience begins at the front door. Ensure all areas indicate what to expect inside. Keep the parking area free of debris, the sidewalk swept, and the windows and doors clean. Inside, dust, vacuum, mop, and sweep as needed. Be the shinning WOW example of businesses in your market area. There is no cost involved other than time and effort. The payoff can be extraordinary. Often we were complimented not only on the cleanliness of the store but also how fresh it smelled.

I once visited a store that evidently missed including cleaning in their business plan. Not only could I have written my name on a shelf, when I was at the checkout counter, the credit card machine was covered with grime. I did not want to use it. My last experience with the business gave me a very negative lasting impression. Be sure the last impression you leave a customer with is one you are proud of.

MAXIMIZING MARKET POTENTIAL

BUSINESS HOURS

Establish days and business hours that will accommodate the market place and maximize the potential to accrue sales. Be consistent about the days and hours you are open. Varying when you are open or closed at a whim will confuse the customer resulting in potentially lost business. If your sign says open to 5:00PM, be open until then. If you need to stay late, do it.

One day we had just closed but were waiting for our delivery crew to arrive to make some deliveries that were scheduled. A car drove up and the man got out and asked if we were still open. We said we were closed but how could we help. Long story short, he spent a considerable sum of money on furniture and other items. We might have lost this business had we closed early discounting the fact we were still there for another reason.

On another occasion, a new well to do out of town customer we had been communicating with told us that their moving van would arrive late in the day and that a lot of furniture on it would not fit into their new home. Could we accommodate them? We of course said yes. When the moving van pulled into our parking lot about 6:00pm, we stood in amazement at the size of the tractor trailer truck. It was huge. The furniture we unloaded was absolutely beautiful. We even sold some of the furniture while unloading the truck. Don't ever underestimate the value of providing exceptional WOW service.

Don't forget social networking. Ask customers and consigners for their email address. Use this information to let them know about your specials, and when something new arrives including pictures, copy, and pricing. The consigner sheet sample I have provided has a place to put the consigner's email information.

DISPLAYS AND VISUAL APPEARANCE

A no cost way to set you apart from your competition is to have a WOW showroom that will not only say you care but will get your customers excited. Arrange furniture, lamps (lighted), knick-knacks, pillows, etc. so the customer can have a visual idea of what the items will look like in their home. This can also set the stage to sell multiple items. They buy the furniture and often times the related items in the setting.

Once a lady told me that the reason she bought the sofa, love seat, end tables, lamps and knick-knacks was because she could visualize how it would all look in here home including the lighted lamps. We, and a small crew that we had come in periodically or as needed, used our combined visual appearance skills to re-arrange the inventory to create almost showroom quality settings. It was always worth the added time and minimal additional expense for the "as needed" crew.

The strip center our store was located in had an overhang that protected the sidewalk from the elements. Every day we would take small furniture and numerous other items outside and place them on the sidewalk up next to the building. Not only was the merchandise visible from the road, those customers coming to the store would first look through all the merchandise before entering the store. Many sales were made from our outside displays. It was also a great place to put discounted merchandise.

If you install glass top jewelry counters or towers, make sure the cases are lighted. Clean and polished jewelry will sparkle like crazy which is what you want to entice a shopper to browse your jewelry selection. Dark and drab jewelry cases are very uninviting. Take the time to step back and look at your display. If it is unappealing, make whatever changes are necessary to create the WOW factor. We sold a lot of jewelry because our displays were well lighted and cleaned constantly to remove smudges on the glass. They were showpieces that virtually every customer visited. It is so easy to do and the returns on your investments can be phenomenal.

I used to smile when a happy customer walked out the door with a small bag tucked away in their purse that contained a jewelry item we had sold that put several hundred dollars of profit in the cash register. Learning the difference between 10k, 14k, and 18k gold and different stones does require time. You can buy inexpensive jewelry books and gold testing kits to educate yourself about precious metals and stones. Another suggestion is to make friends with a local jeweler to assist you, including selling price ranges.

SHOPPING SAFETY
Make sure all aisles are easy to navigate, void of any potential hazard, and that they allow the shopper to easily view the inventory. This is also important to consider for your handicapped customers. It's a vital part of the WOW shopping experience. Negligence could possibly result in a lawsuit. Many stores I visited never gave this any thought. Avoid any possibilities as much as possible and also seriously consider liability insurance which is usually not that expensive. I suggest this insurance be a part of the budget you develop. Better safe than sorry.

PRODUCT LABELING/IDENTIFICATION
Use a price tag system that makes it convenient for the customer to see the price clearly and quickly. If there is anything special about any item, make note of it on the price tag or use another form of printed information to let them know. This can be your silent salesperson. When we were very busy, we actually had customers who removed the tags and brought them to the front counter so no

one else could buy the items while they continued to shop. That was because of the WOW factor throughout our store. From quality to display appearance they knew from experience how quickly our Wow inventory turned.

The tags used in our store included string tags (purchased on the web) and bright yellow small labeling tags that were purchased from a company that provided business store supplies. The string tags were an assortment of bright yellow, pink, and green that stood out on each item we labeled. A permanent marker was used for the information on the tags to ensure there was no smudging. Adhesive tape and a tagging gun were used to affix the sales tag to the items.

For the larger furniture such as sofas and table and chairs, use signs that are contained in a clear acrylic sign display that can be purchased from a store supply warehouse. Not only will they look good, the amount of room to write descriptive information on the sign can help make the sale. Later you will learn where to purchase the signs and sign holders. The use of color markers will improve sign appearance.

Be very careful where you place the sale tag on wall art. If the art is encased in glass, put the tag on the glass centered near the bottom. It makes it easy for a customer to see the price if the art is hung higher on a wall. For art in a frame with no glass, do not tape the tag to the frame. You could damage the frame when you take the tag off. Preferred is a string tag that is taped to the back side of the bottom of the art so the price tag hangs just below the frame.

PRICING MERCHANDISE

Every item in your store has to have a selling price on it. To set the price, there are numerous sources and guidelines you can use to set a price that will attract sales and at the same time, satisfy the consigners. For instance:

Items that are received in the original box that have a printed retail price on them can usually be priced for about one half the original selling price. If it is a vintage item, use the internet to see what they are selling for. E-Bay is a good internet source. If you do use E-Bay, use the sold information, not the asking price information. The asking price and sold price are often entirely different. On numerous occasions consigners would bring merchandise in and say it was selling for such and such on E-Bay. Seeing the actually selling price was always a surprise to them. This also sends a subtle message that you are well educated about your business.

To price furniture, ask the consigner what they paid for it. The selling price would be from one fourth to one half the original cost, depending on uniqueness and quality of the merchandise. If the original price is unavailable, find the brand name on the merchandise and look it up on the internet. Also, look at furniture ads in your newspaper, or visit furniture stores to get a benchmark as to pricing at the retail level. Over time, you will gain the knowledge as to price ranges to consider. Don't be intimidated.

For lamps, knick-knacks, bedding, pillows, etc., use the same electronic, printed, or personal resources for learning original costs and then apply the one fourth to one half of original cost factor to set the selling price. Keep in mind that setting the selling price is not rocket science. It is simply a matter of offering quality merchandise at a price considerably less than what it originally sold for based on logical research.

We also used bound books we bought at a garage sale and those brought in by consigners that focused on antique crystal, pottery, and glassware as guidelines. We even tapped into knowledge some of our consigners had about specific items such as vintage glassware. They welcomed the opportunity to help us.

PRE-SELLING

Pre-sell whenever possible. If a shipment of merchandise is to arrive soon, let your customers know. Provide descriptions and if possible pictures on an inside or outside sign. It's amazing how much can be sold without ever entering the store.

There was one particular instance involving a truck load of rattan furniture we had just picked up. The truck was backed up to the store so we could clean and unload the furniture and other items. We did this often so incoming customers could see the new merchandise. A WOW factor we used quite often. A gentleman and his wife were looking inside the truck and asked if the items were for sale. I told them everything on the truck was for sale and explained that we had emptied out two rooms from a house from the walls to the floor. They stood there for a minute and then asked, "How much for everything?" Since I had inventoried everything when I first looked at the merchandise, I grabbed the consigner sheet, added all the items up and gave them a price including delivery charges. The next words I heard were, "We'll take all of it."

After the sale I learned this couple bought mobile homes, fixed them up and either sold them furnished or rented them furnished. There were numerous times afterwards that we had a great day of sales because they came back again and again.

GENERAL MERCHANDISE HOUSEKEEPING

Keep all merchandise inside sparkling clean. Every item that was placed on our showroom floor was cleaned first. Lamp shades were dusted, tables were waxed and polished and crystal and other glassware was cleaned to an appearance of new. This helped tremendously when we would take an area each day and spend a little time dusting and wiping off the displays and merchandise. The cleaning solution we used on most items was a brand name household window glass cleaner. It did the job without damaging any item and there were no offensive odors. The use of white terry cloth rags was a part of the regiment also. These rags are typically available from an auto parts or big box hardware retailer. The WOW comments regarding cleanliness you will receive are well worth the time spent.

Many times our customers would say "You have hundreds of items. How do you keep everything so neat and clean? This is the cleanest store I have been in." Jokingly we would say that every Tuesday volunteers would come in, they would get a white cleaning rag, a cold soda, and a fresh baked chocolate chip cookie. Then we would ask, "Are you interested?" A hearty laugh would result from the conversation.

Comments from customers provide insight as to how well you are operating your business. The comments we often heard about our cleanliness and overall store appearance let us know we were exceeding what they expected.

SMART MERCHANDISE ORGANIZATION

Many customers that enter your store will inquire as to whether or not you have a specific item. To save time and assist their search, create areas or rooms that focus on specifics such as bedding or cooking items. Bedding, for instance, would be the place for blankets, comforters, throw pillows, bedroom knick-knacks, boudoir lamps, etc. The cooking area could contain pots and pans, aprons, utensils, dish sets, baking dishes, unique cooking items, etc...

The whole idea is to create a WOW setting that not only is interesting, but a place where there are multiples of items to stimulate impulse purchases. The more you can entice the customer to spend time looking, the more likely the possibility of a purchase. Plus, specialized areas are easy to quickly inventory to see if you need to focus on trying to get more like merchandise. If it is spread throughout the store, you and the customer have to put forth extra effort. Eliminate wasted time as much as you can.

AMBIANCE

When a customer first enters the store, the lighting they experience can have a dramatic WOW effect on their perceptions. If it is warm and inviting, they want to see more. Fluorescent lighting does illuminate an area but it is not a warm inviting light. Using track lighting and lighted consigned lamps, the dynamics of any given area can be completely changed. Both types of lighting can be used to highlight specifics such as wall art or a special display area.

Warm well lit areas have a tendency to attract attention. Use your inventory lighting to your advantage to create that special ambiance. And don't worry about the expense to have lighted lamps. Using the new bulbs that are now being sold, a 14 watt bulb will put out the same light as a conventional 60 watt bulb. Using the new bulbs, 13 lamps can be lit compared to only 3 using the old 60 watt bulbs. And the new bulbs are cool to the touch. A good safety feature.

We sold a lot of lamps. The main reason was because in addition to quantity of inventory, we kept as many lamps lighted as possible, especially the Tiffany style. Often times the color of the shade is different when the lamp is lit too. You'll be amazed how sales improve when you turn the switch on.

Even after business hours, we left a few consigner lamps lighted so our inventory could be seen through the storefront windows. On numerous occasions customers would come in and say they saw something of interest after we were closed. One customer taped a note to our door requesting we hold a dinette set until she arrived the next morning. She bought it. For the few cents it cost to illuminate your inventory, just do it.

Another part of the ambiance WOW factor is the pleasant aroma you can create inside the store. Whatever you do make sure it is subtle. We used fragrant scented wax, the kind heated by a high intensity bulb. Never use a candle not only for fire safety reasons but also because if any customer in the store is using an oxygen supplier, you don't have to worry about endangering them. Flames and oxygen can be explosive.

Also as part of the store's ambiance, keep the temperature of the store so that it will be pleasing to the customer. Remember, one of the objectives is to keep the customer in the store as long as possible. If it is too hot, because you are trying to conserve on your electric bill, that is the wrong decision. They will be in and out of the store in a flash. The same is true if the store is too cold. We've all experienced hot and cold stores. Think back as to how you reacted. It is simply not smart to create a negative shopping environment by restricting the use of your heating and air conditioning system. If you think you have to curtail this expense to keep the business open, dig deeper. There is something else going on with your business that requires your immediate attention and correction.

PROMPTNESS

Be prompt about everything you do. For instance, if you have scheduled a time to visit a home to look at merchandise to possibly consign or buy, be on time. If running late make a call. If a delivery is scheduled, prior to leaving your establishment call the customer to advise the customer as to when they can expect arrival of their merchandise. How you and employees conduct yourselves can quietly and effectively leave no doubt as to how you do business. Over time it will create a WOW image that will earn respect and additional business because satisfied customers will talk to their friends about you.

PURGING DATED INVENTORY

Periodically old inventory that has been left by consigners will need to be purged from the store to make room for new items, and to rid the store of items customers continually see. It can either be donated to a worthy cause (consider giving the donated ticket and value of merchandise to the consigner for their tax deductions), or you could schedule and advertise a big "sidewalk sale" to draw a crowd. This type of sale typically attracts people looking for a real WOW bargain so price it to sell. Our sidewalk sales always drew large crowds. The parking lot would be packed. Whatever you get for it is found money. If anything is left over after one or two sales events, consider donating it. Space is money. Don't waste valuable space by cluttering it up with unsaleable merchandise.

CONTROLLING THEFT

Theft is a problem with most every business. Because your business will most likely have an inventory of smaller items that can easily be hidden in a pocket or purse, take steps to advise your customer that you have security. You can buy and install your own camera security system and red lettering on white small signs that say "Surveillance System In Use" and place them on the walls throughout the store. We did and the costs are noted later in the book under the heading Fixtures, Equipment, and Supplies.

During our several years in business only twice did we experience customer theft. Both thefts involved inexpensive rings which were taken from a display of rings we had on top of one of our jewelry counters which were next to our sales counter. The display contained about 100 rings that were arranged in rows in a fashion that we could easily detect if any were missing.

One theft involved a young teenage girl who was looking at the rings while her mother shopped elsewhere in the store. We were able to get the rings back before they left the store.

On another occasion, a ring was taken from the same box of rings. Two ladies were looking at them for a while and then left the store. I looked at the box of rings and sure enough one was missing. I immediately looked out the window and saw them drive off. I grabbed my car keys and went looking for their car. They were right down the street at another business. I walked up to them and said bring the ring back to the store. They hurriedly left the store.

Ironically, the next day the 86 year old man, who we saw daily taking his 5 mile walk past our store, came in with his wife. He reached in his pocket and out came the ring that had been stolen. He found it alongside the road just down the street from our store and had taken it home to show his wife. She told him that the tag on the ring looked like the ones we used so they brought it to us. Evidently the thief tossed it out the car window.

The bottom line is, there are a lot of ways to protect your assets and you don't necessarily have to spend a lot of money to do it. In addition to the cameras, signage and having the sales counter near the front door, we also had a monitored system for our doors and windows in case of a break in which occurred only one time. They were caught in the act and prosecuted.

INCREASING GROSS PROFIT

PROFIT MARGIN

Normally, the gross profit you make is the difference between what you pay the consigner and what is left. For consigned merchandise, if it is a 50/50 split, your gross profit is 50% of the sale. Not many businesses can boast about a 50% gross margin and not spend a dime to purchase inventory. And few businesses can boast about a gross profit from a sale that can substantially exceed 100%. You can with your WOW consignment store. It's easy and you can still be very competitive with your pricing. Here's how.

Often individuals bring in merchandise looking to make a quick sale because they need the money as soon as possible. Or a lot of times they are moving to a new city and just want to unload as much as possible. You will also have occasions when you go to look at furniture in a home that they do not want to consign. They want to sell it. What you do for any circumstance is first ask what they want for it. If the price is really low, grab it. If not, negotiate a figure that you are comfortable with. If they accept, fine. If not, take a pass on the merchandise. There will be many more lucrative opportunities. The whole objective is to accrue quality merchandise at a cost so you can price it to significantly improve your overall gross profit margin.

Now you own the reduced cost merchandise, you sell it, and you get to keep all the profit. Imagine what your gross profit margin might be if say 30%-50% of the merchandise in the store is owned by you. Many times the gross profit we made on purchased merchandise exceeded well over 300%. Not many businesses can make that kind of WOW gross profit. We actually had days that the gross profit from the sales of merchandise we owned was enough or almost enough to pay the rent for the month.

LAY-A-WAY

Sometimes people need a little help to pay for items they want. We found this to be true at our store. It might be a sofa or table and chairs or even a nice piece of jewelry. To accommodate these customers, we set up a very simple lay-a-way system. We purchased 3 part carbonless order pads from an office supply store. The reason for a 3 part pad was because, the original was for us, one copy for the customer, and one part for our delivery crew in case a delivery would be necessary. These were always kept in a safe place just like the 3 ring binders for our consigner sheets.

When a purchase was made, the order sheet was filled out with all their personal information (name, address, phone number), a description of the item(s) being purchased, the cost of each, and then totaled including tax. We then noted the amount of their deposit and the remaining balance. Of course we set parameters for paying it off, especially if it involved furniture because we did not want to tie up floor space for a long time until the merchandise was paid off. We made the sale, the customer was very happy, and even the consigner worked with us. WOW! What we basically did was expand our opportunities to make a sale without making virtually any investment. Christmas lay-a-ways for jewelry was a great way to generate significant revenue.

A WISH LIST

Keeping a "wish list" book is an important tool to not only help your customers as much as you can but to stimulate future business. The book is used to note items customers have an interest in purchasing that are not part of your current inventory. Simply enter their name, contact information, and what they are seeking. If you obtain the item(s), make the call and advise them as to what has arrived and that you will hold it until they come in.

There were times that we would call other consignment stores to inquire as to whether or not they had the item(s) the customer was seeking when nothing was due to arrive at our store. If another store had what the customer was looking for, we let the customer know. Granted, we did not make the sale but it helped the customer and they appreciated it and we still retained them as a customer because of our extra effort to help them.

This is actually a "no cost" way to keep in touch with your customers and to further the growth of your business. A little up front time can often result in substantial WOW increased sales in addition to building WOW customer relationships. Also, a great working relationship was created with other consignment stores. They reciprocated by sending customers to our store if their customer needed something they did not have. Making the initial sale is great, but helping a customer beyond what they expect will always help in developing a relationship that will have them returning to your store many more times.

CREATING BUSINESS AWARENESS
Creating awareness about your business to gain new customers should always be a priority. Like any business, there will be a loss of regular customers for a myriad of reasons. To gain new customers without spending a lot of money there are several avenues to travel.

A good source of exposure is your local Chamber of Commerce. Become a member. Most chambers have a web site that new residents visit. Participate in any community activity they sponsor. Get to know other chamber members so they could recommend you and vice-versa.

Your personal vehicle can be a rolling WOW billboard. Magnet signs on your vehicle can attract a lot of attention. We gained an excellent new consigner by having a brief conversation at a stop light. She introduced our store to several of her friends. All from a sign on the door of a vehicle!

Existing customers are an excellent source for new customers...their friends. Schedule a wine and cheese "Thank You" evening at your store for your customers. Tell your customers to invite their friends.

A business card size or a 1/4 page ad in a local direct mail product that targets your trade area is the desired. Primarily because it gets into the mailbox and also because they are typically saturation vehicles....everybody receives it. Subscription daily newspapers usually have a market penetration in the range of 40%-50%, which means a lot of households will not get your message. Sometimes they do offer a saturation product. Something you will have to check out in your area. Advertising in something that does not get into all the homes should be scrutinized very carefully. Questions you should always ask include:

1) What is your market penetration?

2) Do you have an advertiser I can speak with about their responses?

3) How long has your advertising product been in the marketplace?

4) What pricing options do you offer for multiple ad placement?

5) Do you currently have similar businesses like mine as advertisers?

6) Do you offer exclusives?

If you advertise with a newspaper, ask if they do stories on new businesses.

EXPANDING
As business begins to flourish, a desire to possibly expand will surface. *CAUTION!!* Only after careful assessment of sales over a predetermined time should expansion be considered. The preferred timeframe for assessment should be at least 24 months in order to compare same month performance. If the assessed numbers indicate a steady increase in sales, with no anomalies, and the current sales volume is consistent enough to easily handle the need and increased costs, expansion can be considered. No exceptions!!

KNOWLEDGE VALUE
As the days, weeks, and months go by, your skills regarding the knowledge of merchandise and effective pricing will continually expand and typically so will your revenue. Consigners and

customers will respect and appreciate the knowledge you apply when pricing. One sure way to gain knowledge is to use the internet to research signed or marked items. Often times our research uncovered facts about items that dramatically impacted the pricing and our profit.

Your knowledge and expertise can also provide another avenue of revenue. There were times we were asked if we could assist pricing some items because the individual was going to have an estate sale. For a while we did it for free. Then what we decided to do was charge to perform this service since none of the merchandise was going to be in the store for us to sell. Our rate was $75.00 for the first hour and then $50.00 each additional hour or fraction of. No one ever contested our fees. In fact they were elated we would be willing to help. As you grow with your business, look outside the box for those WOW opportunities to make that extra dollar. It's found money.

MERCHANDISE RESOURCES

Creating resources to have a continual flow of new quality merchandise is paramount to your success. Great resources are your local real estate offices. They come in contact with a lot of people moving in and moving out. Meet them and let them know what you offer. We had several real estate sales people who, in addition to becoming our friends, used us to help their clients. It was a win-win WOW situation. We never had a half empty store. Usually we were scrambling to find space to put everything. A little token of thanks for the real estate representative such as a gift card for a nice dinner was always appreciated. It kept the phone ringing.

Other resources include garage sales, Craig's list on the internet, estate sales, and your local newspaper classifieds. Using these resources of course requires you to purchase the merchandise. The upside is that you keep all the profit and typically what you can sell it for greatly enhances your gross profit margin.

Another way to procure new inventory and also gain new consigners without spending a dime, is to place an upright sign outside your front door with a simple message such as "Earn Extra Money - Bring Us Your Unwanted Quality Items". You will be amazed how many people you can attract. The sign and estimated cost is noted in the SUPPLIES section in the back of the book.

Magnetic signs on our vehicles that stated we Buy, Consign, and Sell quality merchandise always proved to be a good avenue of obtaining merchandise.

Friends of existing customers can be very valuable to your business as a source for merchandise. One day a gentleman came into the store and said a friend had suggested he contact us regarding furniture and other items he needed to remove from a condo he owned. Come to find out, he was the retired chairman of the board of the largest household appliance manufacturer in the U.S. His friend told him our store was the only place he should consider to sell his unwanted items. It's amazing what can happen and who you can attract as a new customer when a very satisfied existing customer thinks enough of your business to expose it to the caliber of this gentleman.

INITIAL SET UP
FIXTURES, EQUIPMENT AND SUPPLIES
To initially set up a WOW consignment store there are basics that are a must to have. Most can be purchased from a closed business, a down-sizing business, re-cycling stores, the classifieds, a store supply warehouse and online. The basic items include:

Fixtures

- A sales/service counter that can accommodate a cash register, credit card equipment, and space for multiple item purchases. Be sure there is underneath shelving to accommodate bags and tissue wrapping paper.

Estimated cost.....$200.00 - $500.00 (depending on used or new)

- Display fixtures for the small and medium size inventory. This could include old bookcases, lighted cabinets, shelving etc... The number and type depends on your business focus. Keep in mind that the better they look the more they will showcase your merchandise.

Estimated cost.....$500.00 -$1000.00

Equipment

- A programmable thermal print cash register.

Estimated cost.....$175.00 - $300.00

- A credit card processor. Companies offering the processing services, including banks, either provide the equipment, sell it, or rent it. Visit some local independents to find out who they are using. It's a very competitive business. Carefully read the contract. Sometimes there are clauses that can bind you to their services for an extended period of time.

Estimated cost.....Free - $500.00 and up to own

- A laptop computer to look up pricing comparisons, unique items, and to market items in your area

Estimated cost.....$275.00 - $400.00

- Cookie oven (Otis Spunkmeyer cookie oven available on line).

Estimated cost.....$250.00 - $350.00

- A sturdy two wheel hand dolly and a flat four wheel furniture dolly.

Estimated cost.....$125.00

- A multiple page feed copy machine. Investigate which models offer the lowest price for black ink which you will use the majority of the time.

Estimated cost.....$70.00 - $160.00

- Security cameras and associated signage. Available on-line and store supply facilities.

Estimated cost.....$300.00 - $500.00

$5.00 (6 signs)

Track lighting to illuminate specific areas of the store. Big Box hardware stores offer these at a reasonable price.

Estimated cost.....$150.00 (5 tracks)

$100.00 (bulbs)-

Though not required, an upright safe is an addition to the business that can definitely help secure your valuables like consigner books. Prices online are quite reasonable.

Estimated cost.....$350.00 - $600.00

Supplies
- String sales tags and string less sales tags that will accommodate a tagging gun for the string less sales tags.

Estimated cost.....$30.00 (2 boxes of each - 1000 per box)

- A tagging gun kit which will contain the gun, extra needles, and clear fasteners.

Estimated cost.....$25.00

- Three reams (480 sheets per ream) of white or colored acid-free 20" x 30" tissue to wrap small breakable items for the customer prior to bagging purchases.

Estimated cost.....$50.00

- A package of 100 7" x 11" create your own Sale sign cards and acrylic sign holders.

Estimated cost.....$25.00 (2 boxes signs -100 per box)

$20.00 (5 sign holders)

- One case each of small, medium and large plastic bags for purchased merchandise. Buy them online or from a store supply warehouse.

Estimated cost.....$29.00 (8" x 5" x 16" - 1 case of 2000)

$20.00 (11 1/2" x 6" x 21" - 1 case of 1000)

$30.00 (18" x 8" x 30" (1 case of 500)

- A set of tools to perform minor repairs if necessary.

 Estimated cost.....$20.00)

- Business cards, magnetic signs for your vehicle, and an open/closed store sign. Also consider a lighted open sign.

Estimated cost......$30.00 (1000 cards)

$40.00 (2 magnetic signs)

$29.00 (open/closed sign)

$75.00 (lighted open sign)

- A roll of 30% off and 50% off self-adhesive discount labels.

Estimated cost.....$10.00 (1 roll each of 1000)

- Telephone with answer service.

Estimated cost.....$45.00 - $75.00

- Radio to break the silence and to sometimes put the customer in a shopping mood.

Estimated cost.....$30.00

- Standing markable sign and holder for inside or outside the store. An ideal item to advise customers of specials and other information of importance.

Estimated cost.....$50.00 (includes 2 panels and markers)

- Miscellaneous such as copy paper, pens, pencils, hand calculator, Magic scotch tape, stapler, index cards, file folder for bills, measuring tape, picture hangers, cash register paper, printed consigner sheets, 3 ring binders, 3 part order pads, etc..

Estimated cost.....$100.00

TOTAL OF ESTIMATED INITIAL SET UP COSTS...... $3158.00 - $5178.00

Quite possibly there will be an office supply and other stores in your area to purchase some of the initial set up supplies. A source we purchased many of our supplies from was Store Supply Warehouse, a professional and great company to do business with. A catalog is available. Their contact information is:

Web site...... www.storesupply.com

Phone......... 1-800-823-8887

Items not listed in the above estimated initial set up costs include rent, internet/phone service, security service, cost of legal documents and advice, license(s) and documents required for your area, utility deposits and signage on the store front. These are variables relevant to your specific area. Getting estimated costs for each should not be difficult. You could then add the additional figures to the above initial set up expenditures to have a fairly close estimate of total costs for your budgeting.

As an FYI, we eventually purchased a used 14' foot moving van for about $4000.00 for deliveries and pickups. The signs we put on the truck made it a rolling billboard. It was a great and wise investment. We kept the truck clean just like our store. When the back door was rolled open, the inside was also always clean. Moving blankets were folded and stacked. All moving dollies were secured. Everything about the truck exemplified how we conducted our business. Owning a moving van is a thought to consider that could be a tremendous asset to your business when timing is right.

DECISION TIME

The possibility of owing your own successful WOW consignment store can become reality. It will take financial stability, a deep seeded commitment, and a structured and tested plan to follow. The business practices we used can give you the guidance to pursue your dream with tremendous confidence because they have been tested and proven. All you have to do is apply them.

Starting and running a WOW consignment store business is not a bed of roses. Some days will put you on cloud nine and some days will seem to stretch you to your limits. But always keep in mind that applying a proven pathway to follow will give you the necessary criteria and confidence to excel.

And best of all, maybe, you too will have that one special day, like I did, when you stand back and look upon your business with pride and that feeling inside of accomplishment beyond any expectation. We were able to be very successful with no previous consignment store experience and so can you, if tested and proven business practices are used. Don't hesitate. Get started and fulfill your dream.

My best to you on your exciting venture.

Ron E. Hill

Contact information: ronhillsbook1@gmail.com

www.ingramcontent.com/pod-product-compliance
Lightning Source LLC
Chambersburg PA
CBHW040921180526
45159CB00002BA/560